TO:

A SPECIAL MESSAGE FOR YOU:

FROM:

MELO'S KINGDOM

THULI MADONSELA

with Wenzile, Khulekile & Zedekiah Msimanga

christian art kids

PREFACE

Melo's Kingdom is a dream come true for me. For many years I wanted to extend to today's little ones the joy of the African fables and proverbs that were part of our staple diet when we were growing up. It was only much later, as a grown up, that I realized that storytelling was how ancient societies passed down wisdom, knowledge and values. Fables and proverbs played an important part in shaping our worldview and characters. It is through the fables and proverbs we grew up hearing that we learned and internalized values such as integrity, truth, courage, compassion patience, respect and resilience.

"Once upon a time" was a familiar start to our post dinner storytelling escapades at my house when we were growing up. This was particularly the case during the days when we were growing up under my grandmother's care. I cannot recall a fonder memory of my childhood days than storytime. It did not matter whether the stories were told at home, church or school. We eagerly looked forward to it as we did our chores during the day. I can still remember as if it was yesterday. Wide-eyed we sat in anticipation around the fire in my grandmother's rondavel.

Looking back, I'm uncertain whether it was the interesting stories that were cherished, or the fact that storytime was the only time we could legitimately sit down and do nothing. Stories were only told in the evening. We were told and believed for the longest possible time that if you told fables during the day, you would grow horns. I'm certain this was the grown ups' way to discourage laziness.

Stories and proverbs also opened to us a portal to lands far away. Because virtually all the stories were about animals. We got to learn about the magnificent variety of animals that roam the African continent. We learned about wise animals such as owls and cunning ones such as foxes. My favorite fable from Grandmother was about Gimba, a boy who greedily gobbled all the food he had been sent to collect. From my father it was how the fox lost its tail. And from my mother, it was the fox that aided a scorpion and the greedy dog that lost a bone in its mouth as it tried to wrestle a bone from a dog in the water only to find that that was its own reflection.

The idea of *Melo's Kingdom* came to me during a flight from London as I watched the movie *Christopher Robin*. Our little princess, Melokuhle, "Melo", my first biological grandchild, had just arrived with much fanfare. My first gift to her was a giant elephant that the mother, my daughter Wenzile, promptly named Nzinga. Incidentally Princess Nzinga had been Wenzile's nickname since she was a baby. This started after my American friend Polly gave her a children's book about the iconic Nzinga, an Angolan princess who stepped up to fight the Portuguese when her weak brother couldn't. I imagine her as Melo's guest whose mission was to remind her of her royal heritage and the importance of her stepping up and claiming her place in the world. The royal heritage I had in mind was celestial royalty that every child has a claim to. But some children are not aware that they are divine princesses and princes hence they settle for a diminished significance in life that others assign them. The big idea was for Nzinga to guide Princess Melo to discover who she is and rise to the occasion having acquired wisdom, the right values and knowledge, through fables and proverbs.

My daughter Wenzile and her husband Khulekile were thrilled with the idea and quickly moved from ideation to project design and execution. Khulekile's father who is a language specialist was delighted to join and Sua du Plessis from Christian Art Publishers graciously bought into the vision. At the speed of lightning the three became fellow travelers and are responsible for many of the enchanting stories in the book. The rest as they say, is history.

Like the fables and proverbs we grew up with, the stories in *Melo's Kingdom* are character-building. Buried in these stories are pearls of wisdom, principles for living a life well-lived and images that transport the reader or listener to enchanting worlds far away. It is my hope that the stories will bring back storytime where families read and tell stories while sitting together.

As a team, we also hope Melo and other little kids will find friends they can relate to among the characters, and wisdom to navigate life joyfully. It is also our sincere hope and prayer that the stories will cultivate God-centered lives. We hope readers and listeners will grow in values such as love, kindness, respect, integrity, self-belief and courage. Above all, we hope *Melo's Kingdom* helps cultivate the audacity to live and lead with authenticity and grace.

Prof Thuli Madonsela

Chair in Social Justice at Stellenbosch University and
Founder of the ThuMa Foundation

MELO AND HER FRIENDS

MELO MEANS "THE ONE WHO STANDS FOR GOOD THINGS".

Through her adventures with her friends and wise lessons learned from Queen Nzinga, Melo is growing into a perfect princess. She is learning to be brave and to stand up for what is right, honest and true. She will make a difference in the kingdom and be well-loved by those who know her.

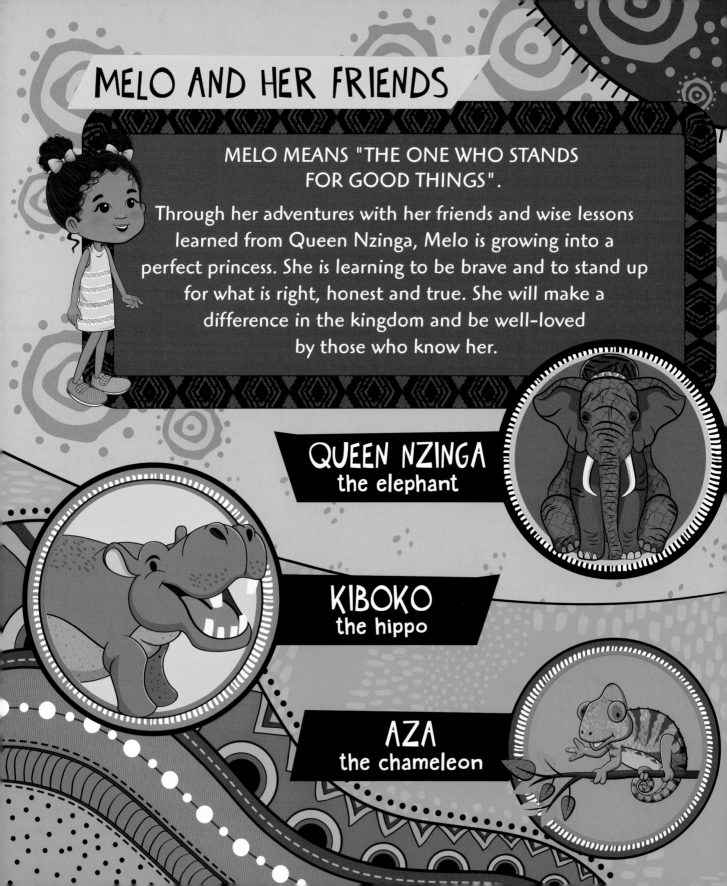

QUEEN NZINGA
the elephant

KIBOKO
the hippo

AZA
the chameleon

ZENZO
the zebra

GANGA
the monkey

BULU
the donkey

TAMBO
the lion

CONTENTS

HOW NZINGA BECAME QUEEN

"I know the plans I have for you," declares the LORD, "plans to prosper you and not to harm you, plans to give you hope and a future." JEREMIAH 29:11

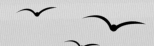

Nzinga is a very special elephant. She is purple and smaller than a normal elephant. She is so small that she can fit in a normal doorway. A day after Melo was born, this strange-looking elephant entered Melo's kingdom with a specific task to fulfill.

The sun does not forget a village just because it is small.

This is Queen Nzinga's story:

"In a land far away there was an elephant king called Nene who was getting old and needed to find an heir to the throne. He had three daughters, but according to tradition only a male could rule the kingdom.

"The king searched the land and chose three young warriors who impressed him the most. The king was known for his wisdom and had a task for the three men to fulfill. He gave them each three seeds and sent them on their way. They had to grow the seeds, and bring back what they had grown three years later.

At the appointed time all returned. The first one brought only one tree with no fruit. The second one boasted fruit from all three trees. The third warrior approached with his head in his hands and explained that despite taking really good care of the seeds, none of them germinated. He had no trees and no fruit.

"The king smiled and appointed the third warrior as the new king. He explained that none of the seeds he had given them had the ability to grow. He wanted to see if they would be honest about their efforts.

"The honest warrior who became king was my father. I was the king's oldest child and he asked the nation if I could be queen after he died, even though I was not a male. They agreed and I became queen.

"At first I did not think I was worthy to be queen. I was small and purple, not at all like the huge, gray-brown elephants in my family. I did not think I was as strong as the men and I did not think I could be a good leader. But with the help of others I discovered who I was created to be and embraced my crown. It has not been an easy journey, but I am respected and well-loved in my kingdom.

"I left my home to come to Melo's kingdom to share my wisdom, and teach her that she was made for a special purpose. Melo is a princess and I am here to help her embrace her role in the kingdom when she grows up. She is princess of a lost kingdom that will be revived when she is crowned as queen."

Dear Father, You've made each person so special and unique, with their own gifts and talents. How wonderful! Help and guide me to discover the plan You have for my life. I want to use my gifts and talents to serve You and help others. Thank You for all my blessings. Amen.

SPOT THE ODD ONE OUT

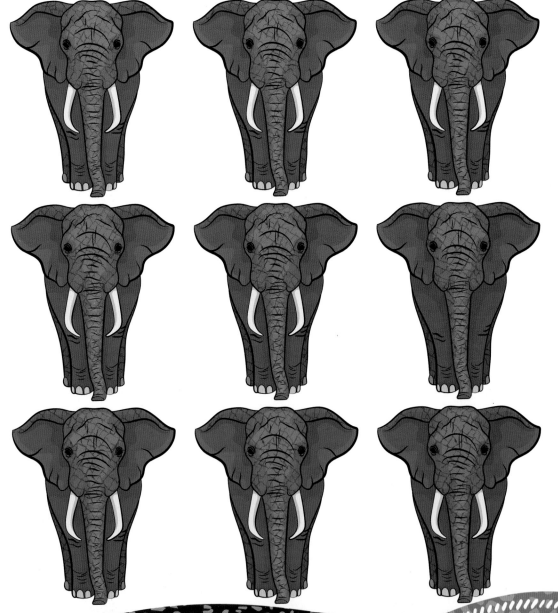

THANK YOU FOR MAKING ME SO
WONDERFULLY COMPLEX!
Your workmanship is MARVELOUS —
how well I know it.

PSALM 139:14

QUEEN NZINGA'S
QUIZZY QUESTIONS

👑 Do you know that God made you special and has a special plan for you?

👑 Have you heard of Queen Esther in the Bible? She was a young girl specially chosen by God to save His people when she became queen.

People judge others by what they look like,

BUT GOD

JUDGES PEOPLE by what is in

THEIR HEARTS.

1 SAMUEL 16:7

WISE WORDS
FROM
NOMKHOSI OWL

It is not by size or outward appearance that we succeed; it is by striving that we succeed. You were made perfectly for a specific purpose.

DADA AND KIBOKO SAVE THE DAY

You are better off to have a friend than to be all alone, because then you will get more enjoyment out of what you earn. If you fall, your friend can help you up. ECCLESIASTES 4:9-10

One day, Queen Nzinga was on her way back from her morning walk. She heard a commotion in the reeds on the banks of the river. She stopped and walked over to where the noise was coming from. Just then the reeds began to shake wildly.

As she walked closer, Queen Nzinga saw Mbeku the tortoise having a serious talk with Dada the duck and Kiboko the hippo. Kiboko had just returned from her breakfast and was her usual cheerful, clumsy self. Her presence explained the wild shaking of the reeds.

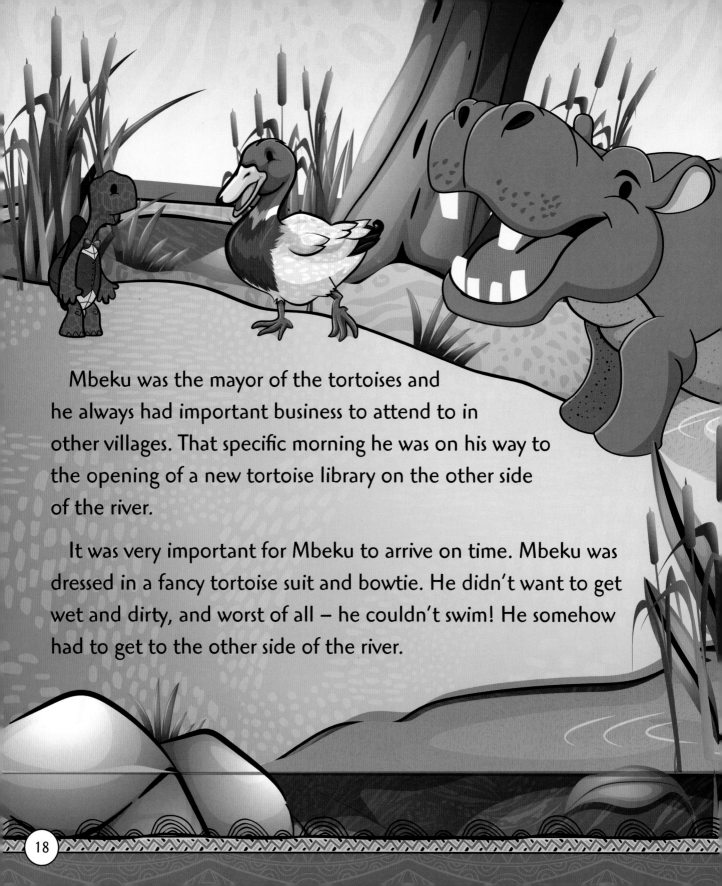

Mbeku was the mayor of the tortoises and he always had important business to attend to in other villages. That specific morning he was on his way to the opening of a new tortoise library on the other side of the river.

It was very important for Mbeku to arrive on time. Mbeku was dressed in a fancy tortoise suit and bowtie. He didn't want to get wet and dirty, and worst of all – he couldn't swim! He somehow had to get to the other side of the river.

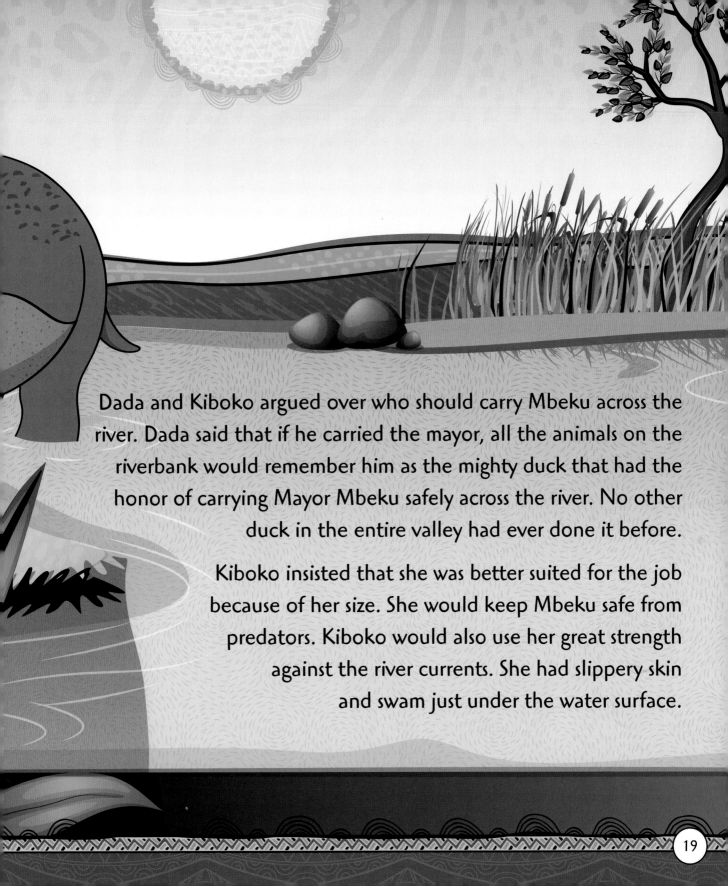

Dada and Kiboko argued over who should carry Mbeku across the river. Dada said that if he carried the mayor, all the animals on the riverbank would remember him as the mighty duck that had the honor of carrying Mayor Mbeku safely across the river. No other duck in the entire valley had ever done it before.

Kiboko insisted that she was better suited for the job because of her size. She would keep Mbeku safe from predators. Kiboko would also use her great strength against the river currents. She had slippery skin and swam just under the water surface.

Mbeku helped Kiboko and Dada
see how they could both help him to
cross the river by using their unique talents.
He chose to go on Dada's back because his
feathers kept him dry while Kiboko
swam right beneath them to scare
off predators.

When they reached the other side, Kiboko ran up the bank and used her round body to flatten the reeds and make a safe, clear path for Mayor Mbeku to continue on his journey.

Dada and Kiboko smiled as they realized that they had both been given different talents that were equally special.

When Queen Nzinga got back to the hut she told this story to Melo and her friends to remind them that no matter who you are, you have your own special talents.

Dear God, thank You for blessing me with gifts and talents to do certain things really well. Help me to use my gifts to do good to others. Amen.

Like Kiboko and Dada, you also have a special talent.

Draw a picture of what you can do well and like doing.

WISE WORDS
FROM NOMKHOSI OWL

When we work together
and use our talents,
anything is possible!

GOD HAS GIVEN
EACH OF YOU A GIFT
from His great variety of
SPIRITUAL GIFTS.
Use them well to serve one another.
1 PETER 4:10

QUEEN NZINGA'S
QUIZZY QUESTIONS

 What are the things that you're really good at?

 How can you use your special talents
to help others?

THE ANT AND THE WASP

Battles are won by listening to advice

and making a lot of plans.

PROVERBS 24:6

IT TAKES A VILLAGE TO RAISE A CHILD.

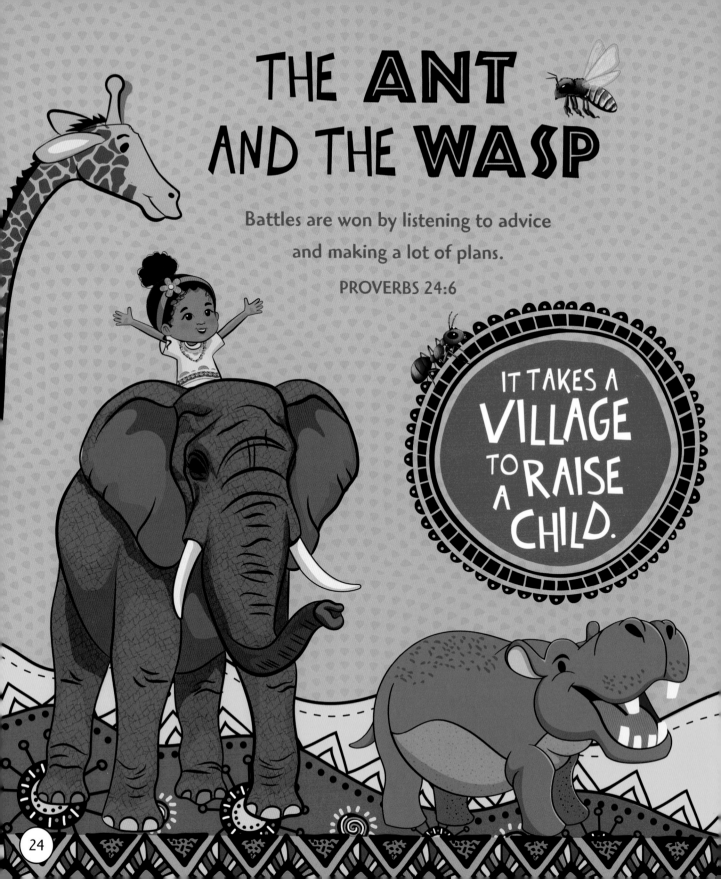

Winter had arrived in the valley. The nights were growing longer and the days shorter. This did not stop the fun, however, because school holidays had begun, and the animals could play and eat all day. One afternoon, Queen Nzinga sent Bulu the donkey and Kiboko the hippo to collect wood for the fire so that all the animals could huddle together for storytime later that evening. Melo was fast asleep, exhausted from bouncing along on Kiboko's back all morning.

All the animals were enjoying a quiet afternoon when suddenly the peace was shattered by much shouting, huffing and snorting not far from Queen Nzinga's hut. As she hurried out to see what all the commotion was about, she found Bulu and Kiboko arguing about how to carry the firewood back to the hut. Queen Nzinga decided that the best way to calm the two friends down was to tell them a story. Back in the hut, little Melo had woken up and was ready for a helping of her favorite storytime porridge.

Queen Nzinga told Melo and her friends the story of Andile the ant and Wasim the wasp.

Andile was a bright young ant who loved to help the worker ants and wanted to impress the soldier ants because he believed that he would grow up to be a big strong soldier. Andile was always up before the other ants and when he wasn't at school in the anthill, he would be studying the worker ants and trying to sneak up on the soldier ants to hear their secret conversations.

There was a wise old wasp who lived near the anthill. His name was Wasim. Andile noticed that the commander of the soldier ants would speak to Wasim every afternoon, but he couldn't hear what they said. Perhaps they spoke in waspanese, the local wasp language. As he grew older, Andile

began to question why the worker ants always walked along the same paths. Quietly, he began to think it was up to him to show them how much more they could explore. In his mind, the worker ants had no idea how much food was out there, just waiting to be collected.

One afternoon, Andile decided to explore new ground on his own. To his surprise, wise old Wasim floated gently to the ground in front of him. Wasim seemed to have come out of nowhere and Andile was quite surprised, even a little frightened. Wasim was friendly and kindly reminded Andile always to follow the paths that the worker ants made. In a moment, the young ant decided he knew better and that nothing bad could possibly happen. He politely thanked Wasim for his advice and continued exploring new ground.

After a while Andile became so carried away with all the new smells and tastes that he lost his way. Suddenly a great shadow came over him. He knew it wasn't the rainy season so he wondered where this cloud had appeared from. As he stopped to look up at the cloud, he was horrified by what he saw. Andile was right in the shadow of a large anteater and it was looking for a snack just his size. Andile knew he had to run but fear kept him stuck to the spot as he remembered Wasim's advice. How he wished he had listened to the old wasp.

The anteater flicked his tongue as he got ready to scoop Andile up into his mouth, but instead, he let out a mighty yowl, leapt into the air and disappeared as suddenly as he had appeared, raising a dust cloud as he ran. Once the dust settled, Andile wiped tears from his eyes and saw a friendly, familiar face. Wasim had followed Andile because he knew

the dangers of the valley and he proceeded to sting the anteater on its bottom just as it was about to eat Andile. Wasim had saved Andile's life.

Wasim kindly carried Andile back to the anthill. Andile will forever be grateful to Wasim for saving his life. Andile knew that he should have listened to the wise old wasp. From that day to this, Andile listens carefully to the older ants and makes sure to learn what he can from their experience and knowledge.

Dear God, sometimes I want to follow my own head, and then I don't listen to the advice of grownups. Help me to listen when I'm heading in the wrong direction. Thanks for always knowing what's best for me. Amen.

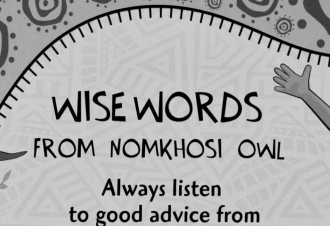

WISE WORDS
FROM NOMKHOSI OWL

Always listen
to good advice from
your elders.

FOOLS THINK THEIR OWN WAY IS RIGHT. BUT THE WISE LISTEN TO OTHERS. PROVERBS 12:15

QUEEN NZINGA'S
QUIZZY QUESTIONS

- What have your mom or dad taught you lately?
- What do you think Andile learnt about life through this experience?
- What does the Bible say about serving others?

ANDILE

HOME

THE DANCING FOREST

God has made everything beautiful
for its own time.
ECCLESIASTES 3:11

A light breeze rose up from the valley. Melo could smell the sweet perfume of the Mfumfu flowers and the damp leaves on the forest floor. She could hear the click-click sound of Insedlu the honeyguide as she leaped from one branch to the next to find a sunny spot.

A tree
does not move
unless there
is wind.

Suddenly Melo heard strange voices. The voices sounded raspy, like a loud whisper. She was not afraid. Instead, Melo wanted to see and hear what they were saying. She walked lower into the valley, and ended up in the shadows of the tall trees. There was no sun at all.

The voices grew louder and clearer. They seemed to come from high up in the branches. She looked up. There was no one there. All she could see were the branches swaying gently in the wind.

Then she heard a clear voice from the branches. The trees were talking to one another. "A people-twig is tiff-toffing this way," said one branch. Then another replied, "Let her come so that she can see our swance." Melo had never heard trees talk before.

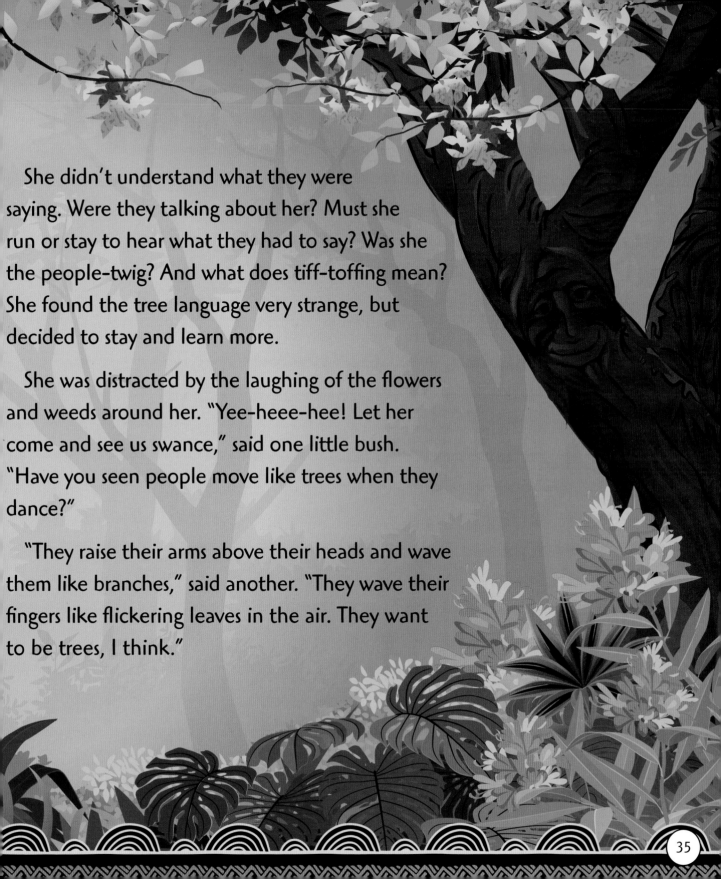

She didn't understand what they were saying. Were they talking about her? Must she run or stay to hear what they had to say? Was she the people-twig? And what does tiff-toffing mean? She found the tree language very strange, but decided to stay and learn more.

She was distracted by the laughing of the flowers and weeds around her. "Yee-heee-hee! Let her come and see us swance," said one little bush. "Have you seen people move like trees when they dance?"

"They raise their arms above their heads and wave them like branches," said another. "They wave their fingers like flickering leaves in the air. They want to be trees, I think."

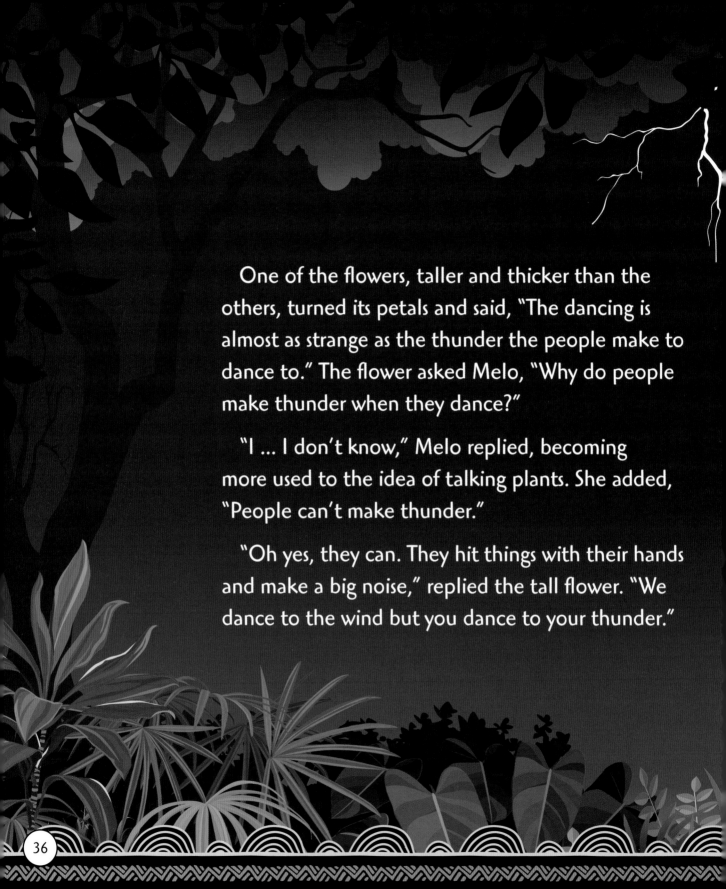

One of the flowers, taller and thicker than the others, turned its petals and said, "The dancing is almost as strange as the thunder the people make to dance to." The flower asked Melo, "Why do people make thunder when they dance?"

"I ... I don't know," Melo replied, becoming more used to the idea of talking plants. She added, "People can't make thunder."

"Oh yes, they can. They hit things with their hands and make a big noise," replied the tall flower. "We dance to the wind but you dance to your thunder."

"You mean we dance to the beating of drums. Tell me then, why do you say 'swance'? Can't you say 'dance'?" Melo asked.

"You see, we swing and sway to the song of the wind, but you thud and thump with thunder as you dance."

Melo thought for a bit and said, "Well, maybe. We beat the drum to make music, not thunder. And we enjoy dancing to it!"

There was a sudden shaking of the branches. When Melo looked up, the tree tops opened up and let in some sunlight. She heard them whisper gently, "Whoosh! Wheesh! Tiff-toff home, dear Twiggy. Mom is waiting for you." Melo heard her mother calling her.

She waved both hands above her head, swancing like the plants as she ran home. The sound of her feet on the leaves made her think of the tree language. She turned and shouted, "Bye-bye! Watch me tiff-toff home!"

Melo thought about all the different plants and animals around her and marveled at how unique and wonderful they were. She thought about the wind moving the branches and making them dance and thought how all God's creatures live and move together. She decided to do her best to look after the earth and respect the creatures she shared this beautiful world with.

Dear God, I want to respect
Your creation, and look after it. Please
show me how I can care for everything
You have made. Most importantly,
I want to love and respect other people.
Please help me. Amen.

GOD
MADE THE EARTH AND EVERYTHING IN IT.
PSALM 24:1

QUEEN NZINGA'S
QUIZZY QUESTIONS

- What would you say to people if you were a talking tree?

- If you could be an animal, what animal would you like to be? Why?

- Go outside and see what creatures you can spot in your garden. What did you see?

WISE WORDS
FROM NOMKHOSI OWL
God made all kinds of different creatures. We must respect them all and look after the earth.

WORD SEARCH

Find the following words:

P	L	A	O	I	D	B	P	L	M
T	U	N	R	L	A	T	T	J	U
A	S	F	E	P	N	Y	W	E	P
M	O	A	O	E	C	W	I	N	D
S	U	N	S	R	E	R	G	M	S
B	U	S	H	E	E	H	Y	E	R
E	N	M	T	U	R	S	U	R	A
N	F	L	O	W	E	R	T	C	V
O	S	U	R	A	M	C	R	S	I
R	B	I	T	N	O	I	T	A	T

SUN

BUSH

WIND

FOREST

FLOWER

TWIG

DANCE

HOW THE FROG GREW UP

Too much pride can put you to shame. It's wiser to be humble.

PROVERBS 11:2

If you are filled with pride, then you will have no room for wisdom.

Queen Nzinga, Melo and her friends were in the kitchen busy baking. Nzinga remembered a story and began to speak:

Once upon a time there lived a frog family – Mrs. Froggie, Xolani and his 100 brothers and sisters. Xolani had reached the age where he needed to leave home and find his own place to live. Xolani feared this new journey, but he did not share his feelings with anyone because he was afraid that he would be judged by the other frogs.

Mrs. Froggie was caring and offered to show Xolani how to make his own home. But Xolani was proud. He lied to his mother and turned down her help. He said that he would be fine – he could go out and build his own home all by himself. Xolani left to start his journey, but he was so unsure of what to do next that he went to the mongoose family for help.

Mama Mongoose wanted to help poor Xolani, but she explained that he was a frog and she was a mongoose and so they could not live together in the same home. Mama Mongoose encouraged Xolani to go home, but Xolani refused and continued on his journey.

Xolani hopped along to the home of the pig family. Xolani explained his story to Mrs. Piggie. Mrs. Piggie was very worried. Still, Mrs. Piggie said that she would give Xolani a place to stay.

The only problem was that Mrs. Piggie was raising piglets. The piglets had such enormous appetites that they ate everything they saw and Mrs. Piggie feared that they would eat Xolani by mistake. The piglets were still learning what was and what was not food for them to eat. Xolani understood what Mrs. Piggie was concerned about. He thanked Mrs. Piggie and went to the last place he could think of – the nest of Mrs. Eagle.

Mrs. Eagle was always friendly and very wise. She asked Xolani what was wrong and Xolani explained his problem. He said that he was sorry because he had been too proud to accept the help his mother had offered him. He said that he did not know what to do or where to go.

Mrs. Eagle laughed kindly and explained that all animals were sometimes proud and that everyone made mistakes. She said that the most important part of learning from mistakes was taking responsibility. That way, one's eyes could be opened to see what was possible when pride was left behind.

Mrs. Eagle was good friends with Mrs. Froggie. She offered to fly Xolani home and he hopped onto her back and they took off into the sky. When they arrived at the home of the frog family, Mrs. Eagle spoke to Mrs. Froggie. Then, Xolani was called in so that, finally, he could be taught about what life as a frog would ask of him.

Melo and her friends did not want to be proud like Xolani. They talked about growing up and asking for advice as they ate their freshly-baked cookies.

Dear Father, I know that the Bible says that too much pride causes trouble. Sometimes I like to brag to my friends. I want to be humble, because that is the wise thing to do. Teach me to be humble like You, so that pride won't stand in my way of learning from others. Amen.

PRIDE LEADS TO DESTRUCTION; A PROUD ATTITUDE BRINGS RUIN.

PROVERBS 16:18

WISE WORDS FROM NOMKHOSI OWL

Learning and seeking wisdom are important for success.

QUEEN NZINGA'S QUIZZY QUESTIONS

- What does God tell us about pride?
- What does it mean to be humble?

SHADOW MATCH

Draw a line from each object to its matching shadow.

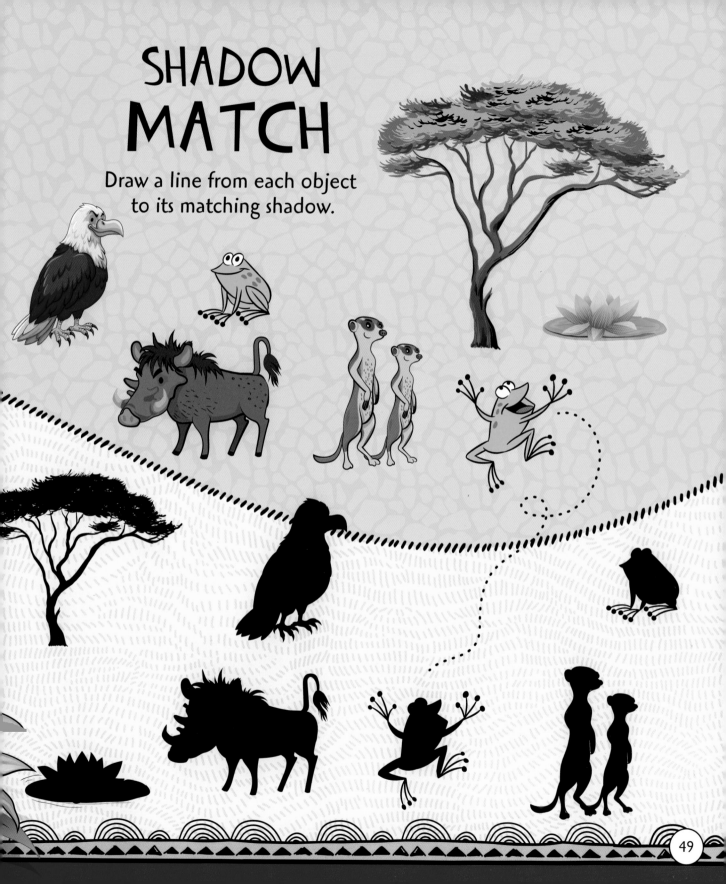

HOW THE GIRAFFE GREW SO TALL

"Anything is possible if a person believes."

MARK 9:23

It was storytime and Queen Nzinga asked Melo and her friends if they wanted to hear about how the giraffe got such a long neck. "Yes, please!" the friends all cried together.

Many moons ago, down in the valley there lived a family of buck.

Those who accomplish great things pay attention to little ones.

In the evenings, Mama Buck gathered the family around for a story and some sweet honey grass before tucking the little ones in for the night.

Mama Buck kept the honey grass in a jar on a high table where the ants and other crawling creatures could not reach it. The youngest of the little ones, Swara, was curious and dreamed that she was tall enough to reach the honey grass on that high table.

Every evening, Swara offered to fetch the honey grass for her mother. "You cannot reach it – you are far too small," her mother always said. As Swara grew, she kept on dreaming of being tall enough to reach the honey grass.

Eventually, her mother said, "Keep on trying, my dear. You will get there one day." Every night, Swara stood at the foot of the table and stretched her neck and dreamed.

One day, Swara was feeling down. "What's wrong?" asked her mother. "I'll never be able to reach the honey grass," Swara replied with tears in her eyes. "Shh now. You just keep on trying and believing you can do it," her mother said, hugging her tightly.

The very next night, Swara gave it another go. She stretched her neck mightily ... And, finally, she reached the honey grass! Swara took a good bite of it and carried it off to her mother. It was the happiest moment of little Swara's life.

"You see, my baby? Never stop dreaming and trying," her mother said proudly. Swara could barely sleep that night. The next day she told every animal she met in the fields about what she had accomplished.

Slowly but surely, animals came from far and wide to ask Swara to reach high things for them.

Swara was loving her new life. She carried on practicing and believing she could reach higher every day.

One day, Swara came home and could not fit through the front door. "Oops!" she cried. "Mama! Why is the door so small?" she asked in a panic. "Ha ha, I always knew this day would come," her mother chuckled. Mama Buck said no more and Swara went to the barn at the back of the house to play with Shishi the sheep.

After they were done playing, Swara curled up on the hay in the barn and it was so comfortable that she fell asleep there.

The next morning, Swara could not stand inside the barn without bumping her head on the ceiling! "Oh no! Everything is shrinking!" she cried.

"Well done, my princess," came a voice from below.
Swara looked down to see her mother smiling up at her. Mama Buck said, "You always wanted to reach up high and you never stopped believing and helping everyone else. Now, look, you are the tallest and most beautiful creature in the valley."

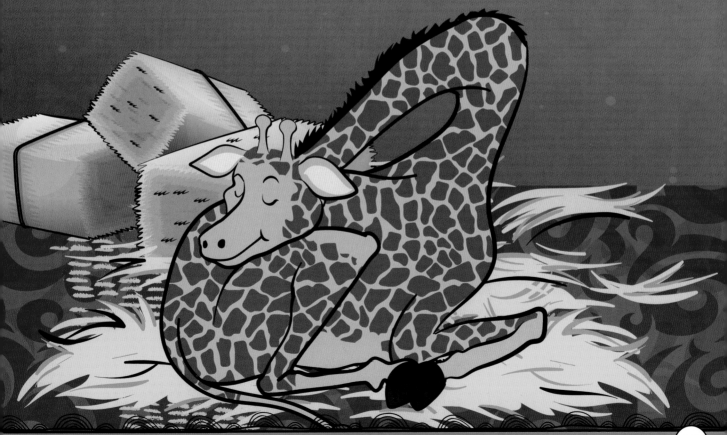

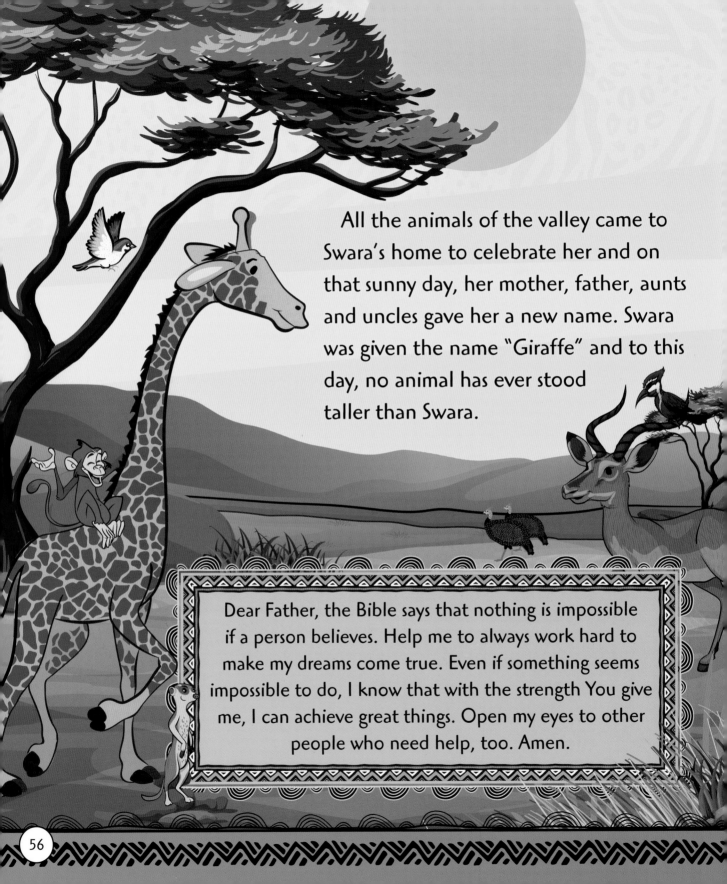

All the animals of the valley came to Swara's home to celebrate her and on that sunny day, her mother, father, aunts and uncles gave her a new name. Swara was given the name "Giraffe" and to this day, no animal has ever stood taller than Swara.

Dear Father, the Bible says that nothing is impossible if a person believes. Help me to always work hard to make my dreams come true. Even if something seems impossible to do, I know that with the strength You give me, I can achieve great things. Open my eyes to other people who need help, too. Amen.

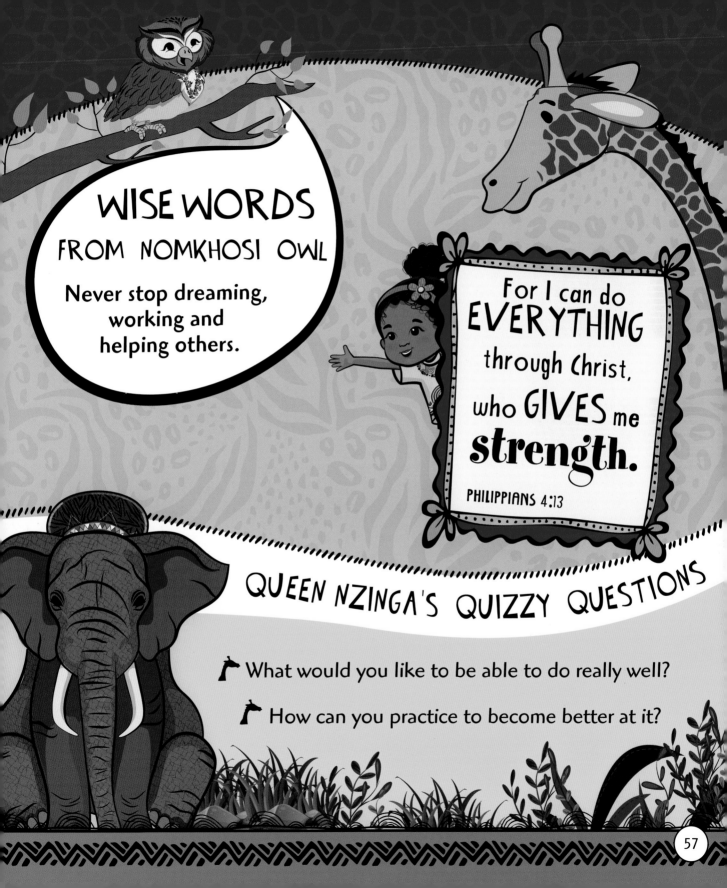

WISE WORDS
FROM NOMKHOSI OWL

Never stop dreaming, working and helping others.

For I can do **EVERYTHING** through Christ, who **GIVES** me **strength.**

PHILIPPIANS 4:13

QUEEN NZINGA'S QUIZZY QUESTIONS

What would you like to be able to do really well?

How can you practice to become better at it?

Find 10 differences between these two pictures.

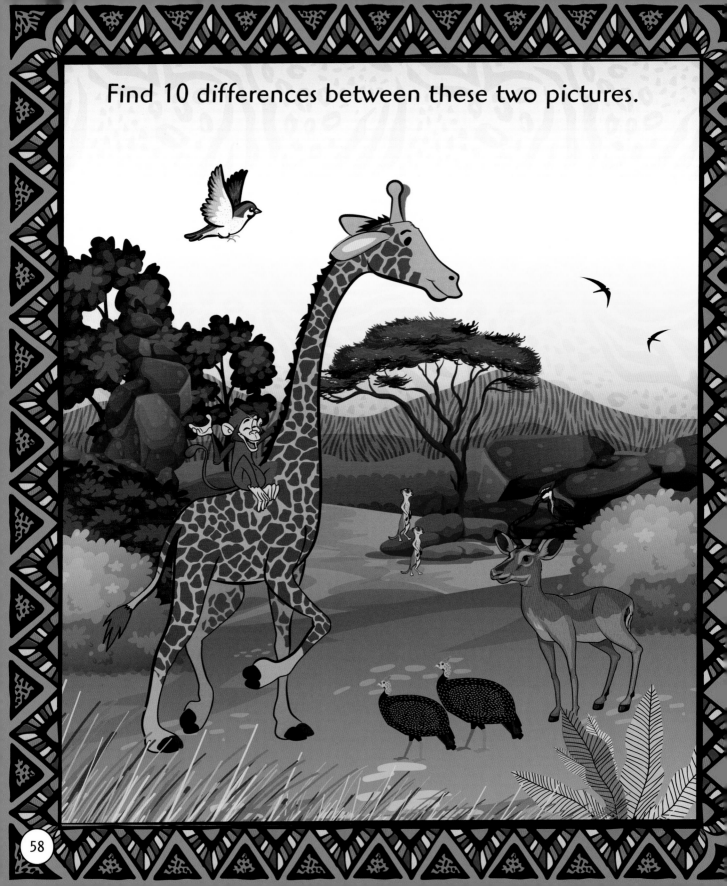

A FRIEND INDEED

Insedlu the honeyguide lived in the forest at the edge of the mountains, close to Melo's home. Everyone knew Insedlu because she always called loudly whenever she saw a beehive. She had many friends and knew a lot of stories about the creatures in the forest.

One day, Melo walked to the forest stream. She heard Insedlu chuckling in the branches of a tall tree. "What funny story have you heard, Insedlu? Why are you laughing to yourself?" she asked, looking up at the bird.

Insedlu flew down to a bush and sat on a branch near Melo's ear. "You won't believe what I heard, Melo," she said. "Some people say they are your friend when they are not. Let me tell you what Hooktail the baboon did to Whitepaunch the rabbit."

Be careful
whom you trust.
Not everyone
who smiles with
you is your
friend.

"What did Hooktail do?" Melo asked curiously.

"One day Hooktail and Whitepaunch had so much to eat and drink that they began chatting like really good friends. At last Hooktail suggested, 'Why don't we have a party at my place this weekend? Then you can tell all of us the rest of your very interesting stories.'

Whitepaunch smiled and said, 'Yes, that would be fun!'

"On the day of the party, Whitepaunch arrived at Hooktail's tree home. It was a huge Mdlawuzo tree. The vines of a Phamba creeper made a net joining the big trees together. The baboons could walk easily from one tree to the next.

"Whitepaunch heard the singing, clapping and laughter up in the thick branches. He called Hooktail and the baboon's voice boomed from among the leaves, 'Hoouh! So you have come, my friend. Come up! We are about to eat!'

"'You know I don't climb trees,' Whitepaunch pleaded, looking up at the smiling Hooktail. 'Hoouh! That's a pity, my friend. You see, on special parties our rules do not allow us to bring food to the ground. It must all be eaten up in the trees.'

'Then can't you perhaps drop a fruit or two so that I can also have something to eat?' pleaded Whitepaunch.
'No, no, no. Only those who are actually at the party can eat the food that has been prepared. We are not even allowed to take leftovers for those who could not come.'

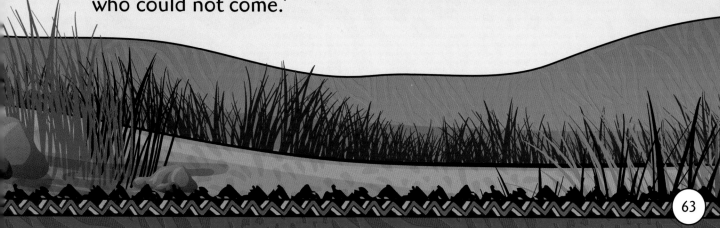

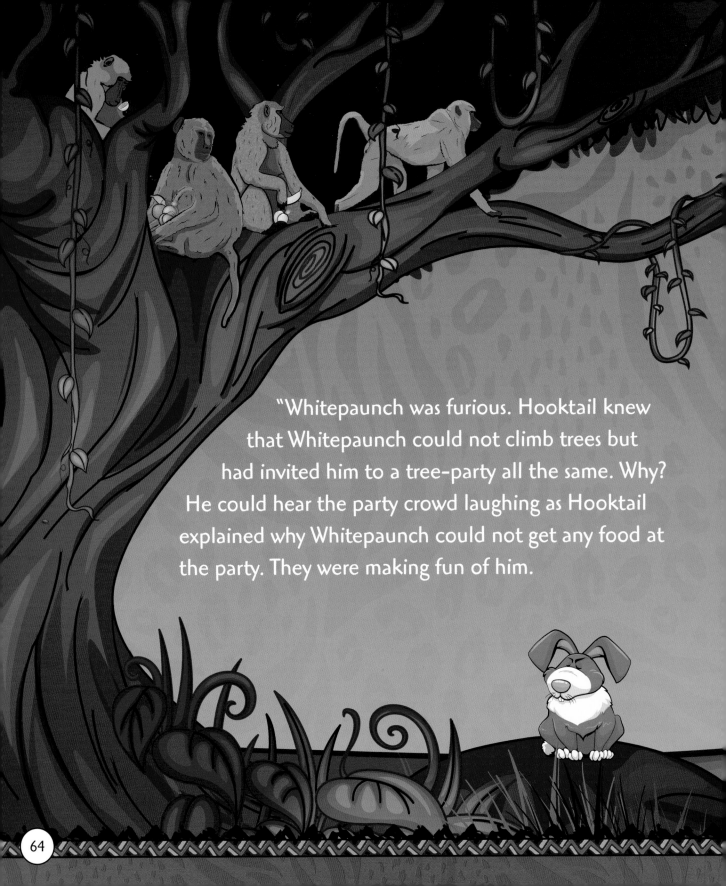

"Whitepaunch was furious. Hooktail knew
that Whitepaunch could not climb trees but
had invited him to a tree-party all the same. Why?
He could hear the party crowd laughing as Hooktail
explained why Whitepaunch could not get any food at
the party. They were making fun of him.

"'Alright, good neighbor. I'll hang around and breathe in the smell of your food and pretend that I'm also at the party.' He hung around the tree trunk until the crowd quieted down. Then Whitepaunch quietly made his way back home, very sad and very cross."

Melo did not think the story was funny. Hooktail had played a cruel trick on his neighbor. Melo asked Insedlu, "What makes you laugh when someone is treated badly?"

"I'm sorry, Melo, but people should choose their friends carefully. I think I should go and find another beehive before the sun goes down." With that, Insedlu flew off without waiting for Melo to say another word.

Dear Father, thank You for friends. Please help me to choose my friends wisely. I want to be a good friend whom others can trust. Amen.

WISE WORDS
FROM NOMKHOSI OWL

To have a good friend,
you need to be a good friend.

A FRIEND **LOVES** AT ALL TIMES.

PROVERBS 17:17

QUEEN NZINGA'S
QUIZZY QUESTIONS

🐰 Do you think Hooktail acted the way a good friend should act? Why do you think so?

🐰 Do you think Whitepaunch will ever trust Hooktail again?

WORD SEARCH

The Bible says a good friend is:

T	A	O	A	W	A	B	I	C	A
R	S	L	F	N	Y	E	H	O	U
U	F	O	R	G	I	V	I	N	G
S	P	V	A	N	M	A	J	S	O
T	L	I	S	T	E	N	S	I	E
W	E	N	Y	Q	B	I	M	D	T
O	A	G	T	A	E	J	L	E	E
R	S	T	I	E	B	H	K	R	U
T	U	V	C	A	S	A	I	A	N
H	A	P	A	T	I	E	N	T	E
Y	C	A	R	I	N	G	D	E	A

CARING
FORGIVING
LISTENS
KIND
LOVING
PATIENT
CONSIDERATE
TRUSTWORTHY

HOW THE ZEBRA GOT HIS STRIPES

Children, always obey your parents, for this pleases the Lord.

COLOSSIANS 3:20

One evening, around a cosy fire, Queen Nzinga was talking to Melo and her friends Zenzo, Bulu and Aza. They were all sitting together drinking tea. Nzinga turn to Aza and said, "Aza, can you please get some warm milk and honey for Melo and her guests tonight before they go to sleep?" Aza agreed, "Yes, Queen Nzinga!" But Nzinga soon realized that Aza had not listened. Then she had an idea.

"Tonight, I am reminded of how the donkey became the zebra," Nzinga said. Melo and her friends gathered around her eagerly, as Nzinga started to tell them a story.

He who refuses to obey, can't command.

Once upon a time there was a donkey family that spent their days grazing in the fields.

In the evenings, Mama Donkey called her foals in to sleep under the tree. One little donkey named Bulu made friends with Aza the chameleon, and they played together long after Mama Donkey had called him in to sleep. Mama Donkey called to Bulu, "Stop playing with Aza the chameleon and come to bed when I tell you to."

Bulu answered her, "I am sorry. I will not do it again."

But Bulu did not listen to his mother. He continued to play with Aza for many more nights. One night, Aza invited Bulu to his house. "Come with me. I have a special drink for you," Aza said, and off they went!

The following day, as the sun rose, Bulu slowly turned white. Mama Donkey asked him, "Bulu, are you still friends with Aza the chameleon? Remember, I told you not to play with him."

Bulu replied, "No, I have not been playing with Aza, Mama!"

Bulu did not know what to do. As the day shortened and the night darkened, Bulu slowly turned black. Bulu was scared. He thought to himself, "I wish I had listened to my mother and not played with Aza the chameleon."

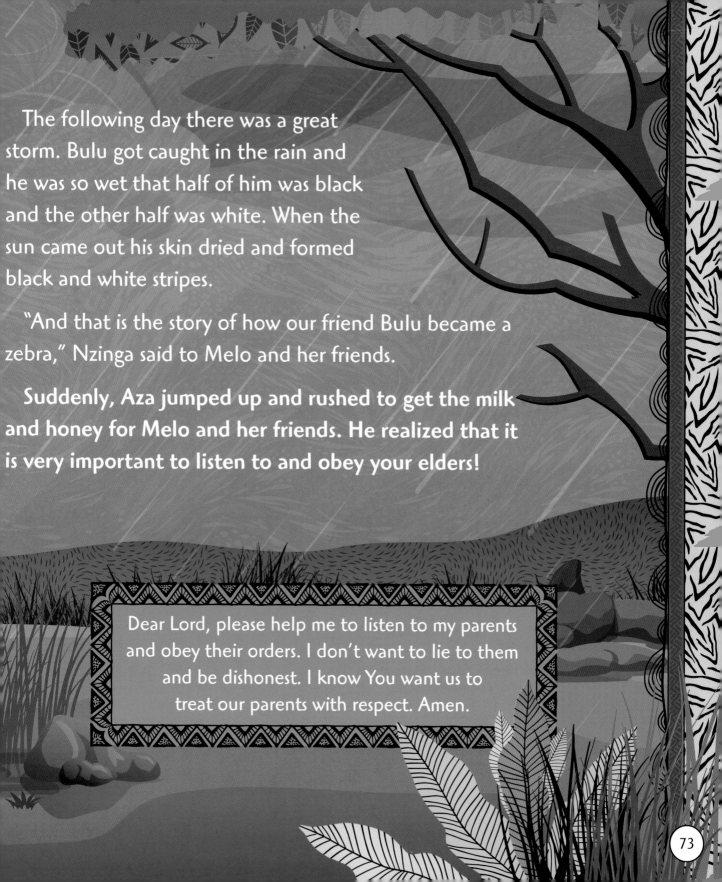

The following day there was a great storm. Bulu got caught in the rain and he was so wet that half of him was black and the other half was white. When the sun came out his skin dried and formed black and white stripes.

"And that is the story of how our friend Bulu became a zebra," Nzinga said to Melo and her friends.

Suddenly, Aza jumped up and rushed to get the milk and honey for Melo and her friends. He realized that it is very important to listen to and obey your elders!

Dear Lord, please help me to listen to my parents and obey their orders. I don't want to lie to them and be dishonest. I know You want us to treat our parents with respect. Amen.

73

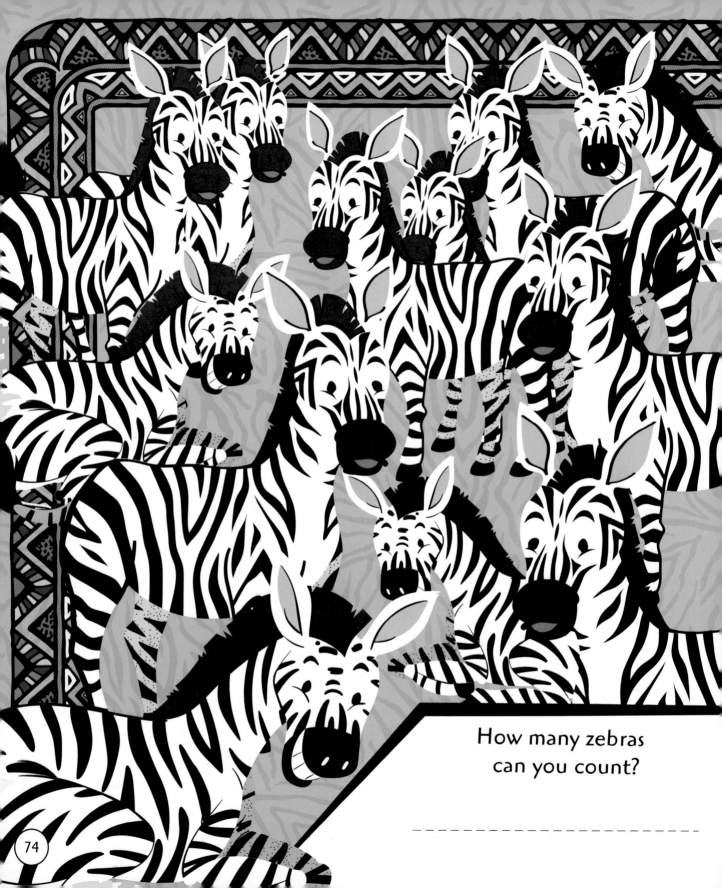

How many zebras
can you count?

WISE WORDS
FROM NOMKHOSI OWL
Listen to those who have gone before you.

> # CHILDREN,
> ## obey your parents in the Lord,
> ## for this is RIGHT.
>
> EPHESIANS 6:1

QUEEN NZINGA'S
QUIZZY QUESTIONS

- Who are the people in your life that you need to listen to?

- What happens when you do not obey your elders?

ANDILE ANT
LEARNS ABOUT HARD WORK

Whatever you do, work at it with all
your heart, as working for the Lord.
COLOSSIANS 3:23

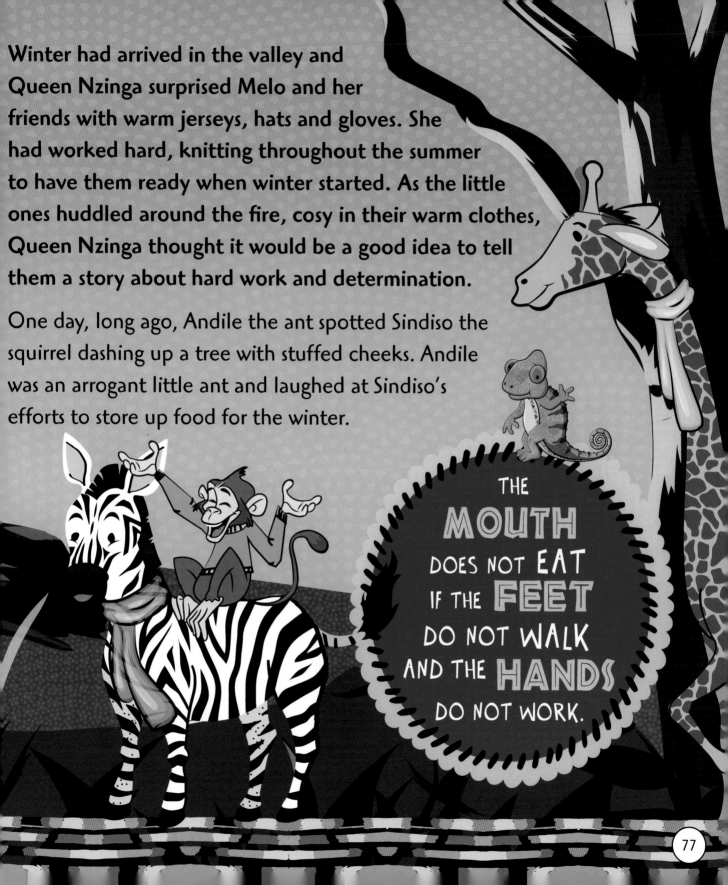

Winter had arrived in the valley and Queen Nzinga surprised Melo and her friends with warm jerseys, hats and gloves. She had worked hard, knitting throughout the summer to have them ready when winter started. As the little ones huddled around the fire, cosy in their warm clothes, Queen Nzinga thought it would be a good idea to tell them a story about hard work and determination.

One day, long ago, Andile the ant spotted Sindiso the squirrel dashing up a tree with stuffed cheeks. Andile was an arrogant little ant and laughed at Sindiso's efforts to store up food for the winter.

THE **MOUTH** DOES NOT **EAT** IF THE **FEET** DO NOT WALK AND THE **HANDS** DO NOT WORK.

"There are other ways for you to exercise you know!" he mocked. But Sindiso ignored Andile and carried on, day after day, quietly running up the tree with cheeks stuffed with acorns and delicious nuts.

As the days grew colder and the nights longer, the queen of the ant colony called an emergency meeting. The colony had run out of food. Andile felt that the future of the colony depended on him. He had to do something! He crawled up the tree where he had last seen Sindiso. "Hello! Sindiso Squirrel!" he called.

The next moment Sindiso appeared. "Can I help you?" she asked politely. Andile felt ashamed because he had been rude to the squirrel.

"My colony needs food, do you know how we could get it to our nest?" he asked.

Sindiso burst out laughing. "What an easy question to answer! Just carry it back to your nest!" she said. Then she showed Andile how she carried food up the tree to store it.

"Thank you, Sindiso! You have saved my colony!" he cried happily. Since that day, ants are always carrying food to their nests and are known to be hardworking and never lazy.

Queen Nzinga told Melo and her friends that hard work and determination pay off. She said, "Whenever we have something to do, we must work hard at it and do our best. We never accomplish anything worthwhile if we don't work at it and never give up."

Heavenly Father, help us to be more like the ants to get our work done. Help us always to be diligent and not lazy when we have tasks to do. Amen.

6 LESSONS

to be learned from ants:

1. Ants are hardworking – they carry more than their weight.
2. Ants work together.
3. Ants don't need a leader – they know what must be done and do it.
4. Ants follow the trail and don't wander off.
5. Ants plan ahead – they collect food in summer and harvest to make sure they don't go hungry in winter.
6. Ants share without complaining.

PROVERBS 6:6-8

You lazy people can learn by watching an anthill. Ants don't have leaders, but they store up food during harvest season.

WISE WORDS
FROM NOMKHOSI OWL

Hard work pays off.

Hard work will reward you with more than enough.

Proverbs 13:4

QUEEN NZINGA'S
QUIZZY QUESTIONS

- Have you seen an ant carry a heavy load? Just think how hard he is working.

- What chores do you do at home?

MATH MAZE

Help Sindiso find her acorn by following
the number maze from 1 to 16.

2	1	5	7	9
↓	1	2	9	8
4	2	1	15	8	0	4
3	3	6	19	16	9	8
5	4	3	11	17	16	18
8	5	6	14	12	15	16
15	7	7	12	13	14	↓
11	10	8	11	10
17	12	9	10	12

83

THE FOOLISH LEOPARD

Keep your eyes focused on what is right, and look straight ahead to what is good. Be careful what you do, and always do what is right. Don't turn off the road of goodness; keep away from evil paths.

PROVERBS 4:25-27

Queen Nzinga, Melo and some of her friends went camping. It was a dry season in the area and there was not much food on the trees.

Ganga the monkey suggested, "Let's drink a lot of water while we look for more food. It can be dangerous if it is so hot and we don't drink anything." Queen Nzinga said, "I agree, Ganga. We must all keep cool and hydrated by drinking enough water."

He who will swallow udala seed must consider the size of his stomach.

As Queen Nzinga was explaining, she gave Melo and every animal friend the same amount of food. The nuts and berries she handed out were meant to last throughout the whole camping adventure. Tambo the lion and Winnie the leopard were not very happy with only drinking water and eating nuts and berries because they normally ate a lot of meat.

In the late afternoon the sun was still so hot that it made it difficult to walk out of the shade. Queen Nzinga said, "Would you all please stay together while we put up camp? It is better if we all know where the others are, especially since nighttime is coming."

Melo and Ganga tried to catch some fish in the nearby stream, lounging in the water to cool off. Meanwhile Tambo and Winnie were getting more and more agitated.

"This isn't fair," Winnie said, "Don't they know I'm a leopard? I need meat."

"I know," Tambo said, "but what can we do?"

"Let's go look for some food deeper in the jungle," suggested Winnie.

"Nzinga said it might be dangerous," Tambo said.

"What are you afraid of? We are the two biggest cats in this jungle, we'll be fine if we go together," Winnie said.

"I guess you're right." And off they went into the jungle, without telling anyone that they were leaving.

Tambo and Winnie soon came across a group of gorillas. Gorilla Chief greeted the lion and the leopard, "Welcome to my land, strangers. Is there something you need?"

Winnie said, "We're hungry and we need meat." Gorilla Chief did not like what he was hearing. He was afraid that the two big cats would try to steal their food or put them in danger, so he came up with a sneaky plan.

Gorilla Chief showed Winnie and Tambo around his land. When they got to a big thorn tree near the chief's cave they saw some juicy steaks. They started drooling at the thought of eating them. Gorilla Chief knew this would happen so he said, "We are having a party tonight and we are preparing the food for a few special guests." Gorilla Chief started talking to a nearby gorilla and they walked off, "I have to take care of a matter, please excuse me." He left Winnie and Tambo alone with the juicy steaks.

Winnie licked her lips, "Can you believe our luck? We can eat these steaks and run away before the chief gets back."

Tambo said, "No, we mustn't. This is not our food. I'm hungry too, but it would be wrong to steal."

Winnie cried, "I don't care. I'm just too hungry to sit and look at this food and do nothing about it." Tambo tried to stop her, but Winnie got to the meat and started eating it. Tambo pleaded with his leopard friend to stop, but Winnie just carried on.

Gorilla Chief was watching from his cave nearby along with all the animals from his land. He had called the animals to safety as soon as he had spotted the leopard and the lion in his territory. Gorilla Chief and his friends chased Winnie beyond the horizon where she was never seen again. The chief said, "Thank you, Tambo, for not giving in to hunger, for controlling yourself, and trying to stop Winnie. Thank you for showing kingly integrity."

Back at camp Queen Nzinga had sent Ganga to find the two cats. He moved through the trees and quickly found them. He rushed back to camp and said to Nzinga, "I found Tambo by Gorilla Chief's cave. Come, follow me."

The campers joined the chief and all the other animals where Tambo was honored for his decision to not steal even though he was very hungry and much stronger than

most of the other animals. Queen Nzinga said, "I'm so proud of you, Tambo. You did the right thing. From now on you will be known as the King of the Jungle because of your integrity."

Melo asked, "What will happen to Winnie?" Nzinga said, "Winnie was given a choice and she chose to do wrong. She stole from Gorilla Chief. Winnie will have to suffer the consequences of her actions."

Back at camp Melo and her friends discussed the lessons they had learned about actions having consequences and about doing the right thing even when no one is watching.

Dear Father God, please help me to think about whether my actions will have good or bad consequences. Help me to act honestly and wisely. Thank You for forgiving me when I make a bad choice. Amen.

Help Winnie, Tambo, Ganga and Nzinga navigate through the forest by matching their footprints:

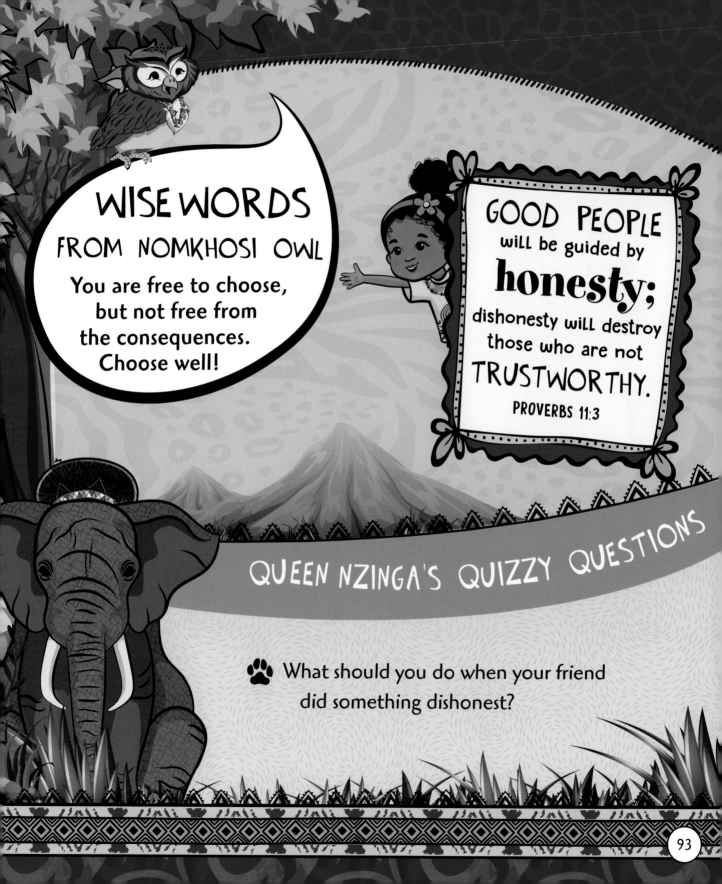

WISE WORDS
FROM NOMKHOSI OWL

You are free to choose, but not free from the consequences. Choose well!

GOOD PEOPLE will be guided by **honesty;** dishonesty will destroy those who are not TRUSTWORTHY.

PROVERBS 11:3

QUEEN NZINGA'S QUIZZY QUESTIONS

🐾 What should you do when your friend did something dishonest?

THE CAUTIOUS CHAMELEON

So be very careful how you live. Do not live like those who are not wise, but live wisely. Use every chance you have for doing good.

EPHESIANS 5:15-17

One evening, Queen Nzinga overheard Melo and her friends discussing how they could get to some fields on the other side of the meadow. Queen Nzinga asked Melo what they wanted to do in these fields and Melo replied, "We want to see the butterflies, there are really pretty butterflies in the fields."

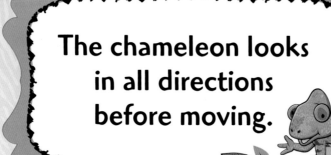

The chameleon looks
in all directions
before moving.

Queen Nzinga knew that the friends would have to cross a
path that farmers use to herd their goats and cattle. The time
had come for them to learn how to keep safe and make the right
decisions. Queen Nzinga called everyone to huddle around the
fire and she began to tell them a story.

Nyasi the grasshopper had just finished his breakfast and was on his way to meet his friends in another part of the valley. As he hopped along, he spotted Chipo the chameleon on a twig. Unlike Nyasi, Chipo moved very slowly and seemed to always be on the same twig whenever Nyasi passed by. "Going somewhere, Chipo?" Nyasi asked cheekily, before hopping off without waiting to hear Chipo's answer. This happened every morning for several days.

One misty morning, Nyasi stopped by and started mocking Chipo for being so slow. Something about Chipo was different on this day. He didn't turn to look at Nyasi, instead he moved his right eye upwards and his left eye downwards. Nyasi roared with laughter and hopped off to call his friends.

He didn't hop very far before the ground began to shake below him. A great dust cloud began to form and before Nyasi could blink, large great hooves appeared and thundered towards him. In an instant, Nyasi felt something sticky grabbing hold of him and pulling him out of harm's way.

Chipo had used his long, sticky tongue to rescue Nyasi! Nyasi was so happy that he began to flap his wings and hop uncontrollably. Chipo turned to him and said in a calm voice, "I am always in the tree, moving my eyes up and down because I always check all directions before I move. Today I saw that the cattle were coming our way. I hope you have learned a lesson, my good friend."

From that day on Nyasi and his friends were always careful, and they played happily and safely in the fields. They did not go where it was dangerous or where they might land in trouble.

As Queen Nzinga finished the story, Melo and her friends promised that they would be careful where they went and what they did.

Dear Lord, I don't want to be careless with the words I say and the things that I do. Please help me to know right from wrong, and to choose wisely. Amen.

WISE WORDS
FROM NOMKHOSI OWL

It is good to think before you act and make sure you do the right thing.

QUEEN NZINGA'S
QUIZZY QUESTIONS

Do you know the saying "haste makes waste"? It means doing something too quickly causes mistakes and time wasted.

- What mistake do you think Nyasi the grasshopper made?

- Do you think Chipo felt like helping Nyasi in the end? Why do you think so?

BE CAREFUL AND ALWAYS DO WHAT IS RIGHT.
PROVERBS 4:26

Queen Nzinga taught Melo and her friends this song to remind them to be careful in what they say, do, choose and listen to.

O be careful little  what you see
O be careful little eyes what you see
For the Father up above
Is looking down in love
So, be careful little eyes what you see

O be careful little ears what you hear
O be careful little ears what you hear
For the Father up above
Is looking down in love
So, be careful little ears what you hear

O be careful little hands what you do
O be careful little hands what you do
For the Father up above
Is looking down in love
So, be careful little hands what you do

O be careful little feet where you go
O be careful little feet where you go
For the Father up above
Is looking down in love
So, be careful little feet where you go.

A FAMILY IS SPECIAL

Follow your father's good advice; don't wander off from your mother's teachings. Wherever you walk, they'll guide you; whenever you rest, they'll guard you.

PROVERBS 6:20-23

If you know his father and his grandfather, you may trust the son.

The sun was burning down so Melo, Bingo, Eggness, Kate and Quacky lay rolling about on the grass under the big tree in the backyard.

"Melo, who was that man who came to visit you this morning?" asked Bingo the dog. Bingo was new to the farm and had not seen the man before.

Quacky the goose started quacking before Melo could answer, "Yes, I saw you bark at him. That was not very nice of you."

Kate the cat chipped in, "His name is Khulu. He is a very nice old man who comes to visit us and tell us stories about things that happened long ago."

"And he teaches Melo all about the animals and plants in the kingdom. And he tells the funniest jokes," quacked Quacky.

Melo finally had a chance to explain, "Yes, Khulu is visiting us for the holidays. He is my grandfather."

"What is a grandfather?" asked Eggness the hen who was busily pecking at corn and calling softly to her chicks to show them where the food was.

"Well, my grandfather is the father of my father," Melo answered.

"And a father is a man with children, like me," Bingo said as he watched his three little puppy sons chasing a chicken in the yard.

At that moment Melo heard her grandfather's loud laugh as he shared a funny story with her mom in the kitchen. "My grandfather is a very special person who is part of my very special family," said Melo with a smile.

She loved her grandfather and all the things he taught her about the kingdom and about how to do things, like fish and catch butterflies. She couldn't wait to find out all the things he would tell her and teach her during the holidays.

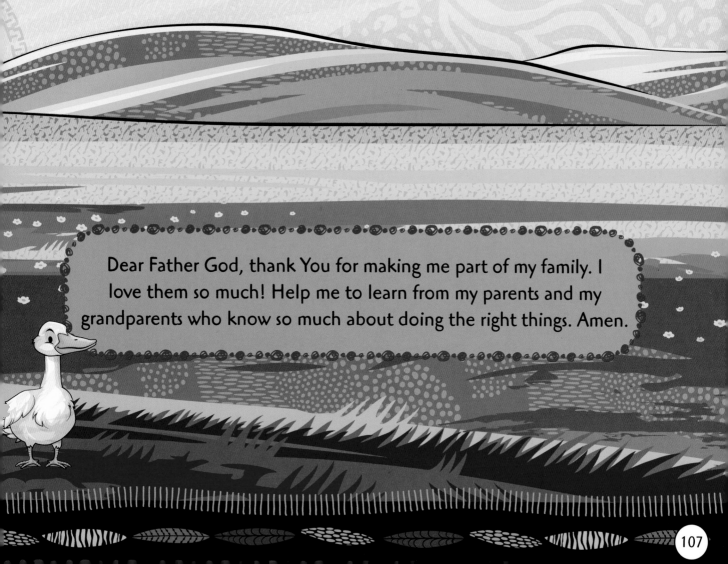

Dear Father God, thank You for making me part of my family. I love them so much! Help me to learn from my parents and my grandparents who know so much about doing the right things. Amen.

FILL IN THE NAMES OF YOUR FAMILY

Grandma

Grandpa

Grandma

Grandpa

Mom

Dad

ME

MY FAMILY TREE

QUEEN NZINGA'S
QUIZZY QUESTIONS

MY FAMILY AND I
are going to
WORSHIP AND OBEY
the LORD!
JOSHUA 24:15

- What do you love about your family?
- What do you like to do together as a family?
- Name all your family members and describe each of them.

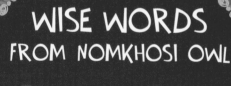

WISE WORDS
FROM NOMKHOSI OWL

Treasure your identity
because it sets you apart
by making you a part
of a wholesome whole.

STRONGER TOGETHER

Let us think of ways to motivate one another to acts of love and good works. And let us not neglect our meeting together... but encourage one another. HEBREWS 10:24-25

Late one afternoon
on a hot summer's day,
Melo and her friends
were playing in the forest.
They were going to sleep
under the stars that evening.
Queen Nzinga called them
closer because it was getting
dark. "We need wood to
make a fire before dark,"
she reminded them.

Bulu and Kiboko eagerly started
gathering sticks. They liked to finish
first when doing chores.

Sticks in a
bundle are
unbreakable.

Melo's friends ran
off without realizing
that they had left poor
Melo behind, all by herself.
She wandered into the forest to
see if she could spot some of her
animal friends.

As she walked deeper into the
forest it became pitch dark.
She couldn't even see the stars
anymore.

When all the animals got back to the clearing, Queen Nzinga looked around. "Where is Melo?" she asked. The other animals were startled, and started pointing fingers at each other. "You should've stayed with Melo!", "No, you should've!"

"Stop! Everybody, keep quiet now. We need to work together to find Melo," said Nzinga. Bulu suggested that they all surround the area and search every nook and cranny. That way, they would be sure to find Melo.

Nzinga was happy with the plan, and divided them up in groups of two. Some time went by, and eventually Bulu and Kiboko heard a small voice crying out. It was Melo! She had made friends with the birds and was imitating their sounds hoping that her animal friends would hear it. And finally they did!

Nzinga congratulated all the animals on working together. She said that they would not have been able to find Melo if they had not worked together.

As the animals walked back to the clearing, Nzinga remembered something that she had learned while she was preparing to become queen. She had been taught that animals are always stronger when they work together. Unity breeds kindness. Melo and her friends reminded Nzinga of a lesson that she had almost forgotten.

Dear God, thank You for giving us friends and family to love and care for us. Help me to remember that I am never alone. I want to learn to work together with others to get things done. Sometimes I want to do things my own way, without the help of others, but I know that's not always the right way. Please help me to listen to others who want to help and guide me. Amen.

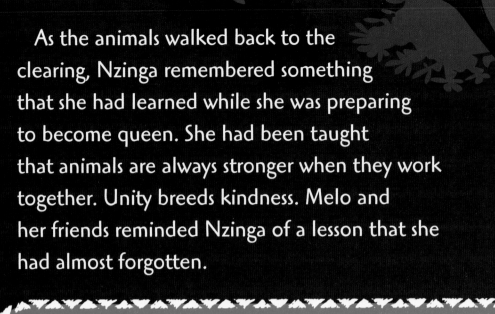

SHADOW MATCH

Draw lines from Melo and her friends to their matching shadows.

AS IRON **SHARPENS** IRON, so a **FRIEND SHARPENS A FRIEND.**

PROVERBS 27:17

WISE WORDS
FROM
NOMKHOSI OWL

TOGETHER
EVERYONE
ACHIEVES
MORE

Alone we can do little, but together we can do a whole lot more.

QUEEN NZINGA'S
QUIZZY QUESTIONS

- When was a time that you had to work with others to get something done?

- Do you think the animals would have found Melo if they hadn't worked together?

MELO CLIMBS A MOUNTAIN

I lift up my eyes to the hills. From where does my help come?
My help comes from the LORD, who made heaven and earth.
PSALM 121:1-2

The brave man is not he who doesn't feel afraid, but the one who conquers that fear.

Melo and her animal friends were going on another adventure. This time Queen Nzinga was taking them to a mountain far outside the kingdom. The special thing about this mountain was that at certain times of the year it was covered with snow. Queen Nzinga wanted to teach Melo that anything is possible if you really set your heart on it, even seeing snow in Africa.

Melo and the animals arrived at the village at the foot of a huge mountain. They were welcomed by the villagers who were friends with Queen Nzinga. She had been a fair and kind ruler to all the animals and people throughout Africa. They graciously opened their homes and the friends were fascinated by the clay houses in the village. Adilah, an old friend of Nzinga, showed the animals around and said, "Tomorrow I have to work in the mountains so I have asked Hakan to be your guide."

The next morning, the sun woke Melo with its bright rays. Although she was far away from home, she was very excited. Melo went to look for the others and found Kiboko and Aza cooking a traditional dish with a few of the villagers.

Queen Nzinga called Melo, Kiboko, Aza and Tahiya the reindeer and said, "It's very important to eat a good meal before you set off. You will need the energy. The leftovers will be packed in for you to take with. Ah, here comes Hakan."

Hakan was a hedgehog and he greeted the travelers enthusiastically. He explained that he had been a guide for many years and had never been disappointed in his trip up the mountain.

He said that his big ears help him to hear when snow is going to fall.

Finally the group was ready to set off. Queen Nzinga stayed in the village to help Adilah. Melo found it hard to believe that there would be snow anywhere nearby because it was so hot and sunny.

Hakan led the group and they walked one behind the other up a rocky path. It was tough going and it wasn't long before the animals started asking, "Are we nearly there yet?" Hakan reminded them that anything worthwhile requires hard work and that if they keep going they will be rewarded.

Eventually Melo grew so tired that Hakan organized a mule to carry her. The sun was at its peak and everyone felt like quitting. Tahiya was used to climbing rocky mountains so she offered to carry Aza. Hakan saw that spirits were low so he sang a song to cheer them up. It worked and the group picked up their pace.

But all of a sudden Kiboko lost her grip and slipped. The path had become wet and slippery from the melting snow. Hakan called the others, "Come together everyone. We are almost at the top!"

Kiboko's fall had scared everyone and the sun was hidden behind the snow clouds so it made it dark and more difficult to walk. Hakan encouraged the despondent little group, "The unexpected always seems scary at first, but once you manage to get past your fear there is always a prize."

The group suddenly heard a cheer from further up the path. Tahiya waved excitedly and called Melo and the other animals, "I see the snow!"

It was more beautiful than they could ever have imagined. Melo cried out delightedly, "It's even prettier than in the pictures!" The animals played in the snow and made friends with the other children who were there.

"To think that we almost turned around and went back," said Kiboko.

"Yes," agreed Melo, "but we conquered the mountain and what a prize awaited us!"

The group arrived home very tired yet extremely happy. Queen Nzinga was glad that Melo had learned how to climb a mountain and conquer the fear within.

Dear God, thank You that when I trust in You, You help me to do things that seem scary and difficult. With You, all things are possible! Amen.

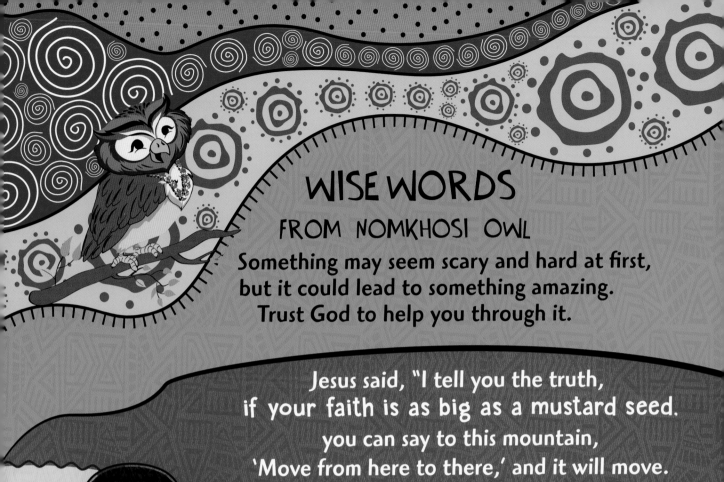

WISE WORDS
FROM NOMKHOSI OWL

Something may seem scary and hard at first, but it could lead to something amazing. Trust God to help you through it.

Jesus said, "I tell you the truth, if your faith is as big as a mustard seed, you can say to this mountain, 'Move from here to there,' and it will move. All things will be possible for you."

MATTHEW 17:20

QUEEN NZINGA'S
QUIZZY QUESTIONS

* When was a time you had to do something scary? What did you do?

* Who helped you not to be afraid?

DID YOU KNOW?

The **African elephant** is the largest mammal on land.

The **hippopotamus** can run really fast, reaching speeds of about 32 kilometers (or 20 miles) per hour. Hippos cannot swim, they only walk or run underwater.

The **gorilla** is the largest primate on earth.

The eyes of a **chameleon** can turn in all directions. The tongue is about twice the length of the chameleon's body so it can catch insects that are quite a distance away.

They may be the tallest animals in the world, but **giraffes** sleep for the shortest length of time – only about 30 minutes every day.

Hedgehogs can swim well and even climb trees, despite their poor eyesight. Their great sense of smell and hearing help them get around.

A **zebra's** stripes act like a fingerprint – each individual's pattern is unique.

Lions have the loudest roar of the big cats. A male lion's roar can be heard from up to eight kilometers (5 miles) away, allowing them to communicate with each other over long distances.

Queen Nzinga's
Peaceful Advice

Words of wisdom make good sense. PROVERBS 15:7

A bird's relative is the one with whom it shares a nest.

Melo and her friends couldn't wait for Queen Nzinga to arrive. She had been called to a country far outside the kingdom. Queen Nzinga was known for her wisdom and her skills to solve problems in a peaceful manner and was regularly called away to help others.

The door swung open and Queen Nzinga stood there with her heavy bags. She was very tired after her long journey. Aza took her bags and put them down while Bulu immediately poured water in the pot to make tea for her.

Melo peeped out from behind Tambo's leg. It was past her bedtime, but she insisted on staying awake until Queen Nzinga came home. Queen Nzinga spotted Melo and gave her a delighted smile and a big hug.

Queen Nzinga could see that everybody was excited to hear about the great adventure she had been on. Tambo had been left in charge of the fort and immediately reported that there had been no incidents, and that everybody was safe and in good spirits. Bulu came running along with a fresh cup of rooibos tea for Queen Nzinga.

Queen Nzinga settled down and started to tell them about her amazing trip to her friend Anna, the ruler of a land with one of the largest lakes in the world. The lake was known for its delicious clear water and the beautiful landscape of the area.

"Anna told me how her land was changing. People had started to put pipes in the lake in order to drain the water and put it in bottles to sell it. She was worried that the water would be polluted by the pipes and factories and that it would no longer be clear and delicious. She was worried that the animals would not have water to drink.

"Some of the people selling the water were part of a tribe that lived in the area but no longer had enough money to survive. They sold the water to earn an income. Anna didn't know what to do about the problem."

Queen Nzinga sipped her tea and continued her story, "I gave Anna the following advice. I suggested that the communities in the area limit the number of pipes put in the lake and share the pipes so that only a certain amount of the water is used. In this way the water and surrounding area would be protected and not misused.

"The tribe living in the area could sell the water to people who came from far away to see the beautiful lake and land. This would ensure that there would be enough water and money for food for years to come.

"My friend Anna realized that things are changing, but it does not have to be a bad thing. She learned that there is a peaceful way to work together for everyone's good."

The group was impressed with the peaceful answer Nzinga had found for Anna's problem. Then it was time for everyone to go to bed. Nzinga whispered to Tambo that the world was changing and they, the young ones, would have the responsibility to change in a way that's fair and just for future generations. She smiled at Tambo and whispered softly, "We never choose war, always peace."

Dear Father, I want to make good choices that please You.
Help me remember to ask others when I need to make big decisions.
I know that I can always talk to You about anything. Thank You, Lord. Amen

Queen Nzinga shows us how
to live in peace with others.
Peace is one of the fruits of the Spirit.
Let's take a look at the other fruits
that God wants us to show in our lives.

Fill in the missing letters to complete the words below.

LOVE, JOY, PEACE, PATIENCE, KINDNESS,
GOODNESS, FAITHFULNESS,
GENTLENESS, SELF-CONTROL

"But the fruit of the Spirit is

L_V_   J_Y   P_A_E

P_T_E_C_   K_N_N_SS

G_O_N_SS   F_I_H_U_N_SS

G_N_L_N_SS

S_L_-C_N_R_L."

GALATIANS 5:22-23

> LOSING YOUR TEMPER **CAUSES** A LOT OF TROUBLE,
> but staying **CALM** SETTLES ARGUMENTS.
>
> PROVERBS 15:18

QUEEN NZINGA'S
QUIZZY QUESTIONS

- Do you know how valuable water is? In what ways can you save water?

- Whom do you go to for help when you don't know what to do? Why?

- Always try to settle a fight in a peaceful way. What do you do when you and your friend have a fight?

WISE WORDS
FROM NOMKHOSI OWL

Choosing peace is the
wise thing to do,
in all you say let God's
love shine through.

ABOUT THE CO-AUTHORS

Wenzile Madonsela Msimanga is a Social Entrepreneur, Mental Health activist and Democracy Defender. She is passionately dedicated to closing the gaps that social injustice creates in South Africa and globally. She dynamically advocates for and is involved in sustainable programs that are geared towards empowering people specifically through enterprise development and mental wellness advocacy. Wenzile is mother to Melokuhle and takes immense pleasure in engaging with childhood development, especially in an ever-changing world. She is a believer in ubuntu, innovation and preserving innocence amongst children.

Having lived in seven towns across two countries, **Khulekile Msimanga** was always bound to have a creative streak. This exposure to different cultures, traditions and languages stirred up a keen interest in storytelling and in entrepreneurship. To sample the best of both worlds, Khulekile trained as a Chartered Accountant (SA) and began using numbers to tell stories. As a proud husband and father to Melokuhle, his contribution to this book is a small way of bringing wisdom, joy, and happiness to little ones everywhere.

Zedekiah Msuthu Msimanga was born in 1948, the third in a family of ten children. He grew up under his grandmother's care from the age of two because Mama had so many children. His school had only grades 1 to 5, only two teachers, and only one classroom in which all lessons were taught. He became a high school teacher, a teacher-training college lecturer, and retired as a university lecturer.

Melo's Kingdom

Copyright © 2020 by Christian Art Kids, an imprint of Christian Art Publishers,
PO Box 1599, Vereeniging, 1930, RSA

© 2020
First edition 2020

Cover designed by Christian Art Kids
Photo of author used by permission from *Marie Claire*
Designed by Christian Art Kids
Artwork: Melissa Vermaak, Leree Henning and Karen Ezzi
Images used under license from Shutterstock.com

Printed in China

ISBN 978-1-4321-3409-9

21   22   23   24   25   26   27   28   29   30   –   12   11   10   9   8   7   6   5   4   3

Printed in Shenzhen, China
JULY 2021
Print Run: 110303